NAVIGATING SPIRITUAL SUICIDE

A Journey to Repentance and Restoration

While every precaution has been taken in the preparation of this book, the publisher assumes no responsibility for errors or omissions, or for damages resulting from the use of the information contained herein.

NAVIGATING SPIRITUAL SUICIDE, A JOURNEY TO REPENTANCE AND RESTORATION

First edition. January 23, 2024.

Copyright © 2024 Dr. Carla McArthur.

ISBN: 979-8224753949

Written by Dr. Carla McArthur.

Table of Contents

Dedication

———

This book is a heartfelt tribute to the remarkable individuals whose influence and guidance have profoundly shaped my spiritual journey. Their unwavering support and visionary leadership have not only ignited the flame of faith within me but have also played an instrumental role in the narrative that unfolds within these pages.

In memory of Bishop L. Ron Sailor Sr., a beacon of faith whose encouragement and visionary leadership provided the platform for the transformative journey recounted here. Your belief in my calling sparked a flame that continues to burn brightly, inspiring me to navigate the complexities of faith with courage and conviction.

To Apostle Gilbert Coleman Jr., whose nurturing of my ministerial training planted the seeds of my calling. The foundation you meticulously laid paved the way for the transformative odyssey detailed in this book. Your wisdom and guidance have been a constant source of inspiration.

In remembrance of Late Pastor, Dr. William L. Gaffney, whose leadership created a community fostering growth, understanding, and a shared commitment to God's divine calling. May this book stand as a testament to the collective journey I persist in, navigating the path of faith that you, in your wisdom, helped illuminate.

To Pastor Mark Thompson, Sr., your open-hearted embrace and wise guidance have allowed me to continue using my gifts and answering the call. Your mentorship has been a cornerstone, shaping the trajectory of my ministry in ways I could not have foreseen. Your support is an invaluable part of this ongoing journey.

This work is not just my expression but a tribute to the faith communities, mentors, and fellow journeyers who have played pivotal roles in shaping my spiritual pilgrimage. May the profound lessons learned, and the wisdom shared within these pages contribute to the ongoing narrative of our shared faith journey

Preface

In the quiet corridors of my personal struggles, echoes resonate with the uncertainty of a hesitant prophet—Jonah. My journey commenced with a sermon titled 'Spiritual Suicide,' a testament to my unique pilgrimage. Surprisingly, it mirrored Jonah's wrestle with defiance and reluctance in response to a divine calling.

Yet, beneath the layers of personal introspection, a more profound purpose awaits this unfolding narrative. As I transcribe these reflections, unveiling the chronicle of spiritual battles and redemption, it transcends mere documentation of my individual tribulations. Instead, it stands as a heartfelt invitation—a call to explore the shared human experience of doubt, defiance, and the transformative metamorphosis that emerges in the wake of God's intervention.

Introduction

———

This book serves as both a spiritual shepherding guide and a personal narrative commentary, inviting readers on a transformative journey from the depths of spiritual struggle to the shores of divine restoration. Grounded in the biblical account of Jonah, the author intertwines personal reflections, theological insights, and practical wisdom to explore universal themes of doubt, awakening, and the boundless compassion of God.

The primary aim is to provide readers with a framework for self-exploration and spiritual growth. By delving into the challenges of confronting spiritual struggles, finding comfort in the familiar, and navigating life's storms, readers are encouraged to reflect on their own journeys. Through the lens of God's compassion and second chances, the book illuminates the path to renewal and spiritual rebirth.

Each chapter invites readers to explore their own experiences, drawing parallels with biblical story and discovering the transformative power of Godly intervention. The bonus section further enriches exploration by delving into the stories of notable disobedient characters, offering valuable lessons and insights.

The ultimate goal is to inspire individuals to answer God's call, confront their spiritual battles, and embrace the journey of repentance and restoration. Through reflections, anecdotes, and a closing prayer, readers are encouraged to seek Godly guidance, acknowledge their shortcomings, and trust in the unwavering love and compassion of a merciful God.

In a world marked by uncertainty and challenges, this book aims to be a source of hope, encouragement, and a roadmap for those seeking a deeper connection with God. It is an invitation to confront spiritual struggles, navigate the complexities of faith, and experience the transformative power of saying 'yes' to God's call.

Unraveling Shadows: Navigating Spiritual Suicide in the Tapestry of Faith and Restoration

In the vast tapestry of human experiences, a silent phenomenon often conceals itself—spiritual suicide. This transcendent force extends beyond the secular realm, infiltrating the sacred spaces within the body of Christ. Year after year, countless individuals engage in a form of self-destruction, not in the physical sense but in a profound spiritual dimension.

Our exploration turns to the scriptures, specifically the story of Jonah, unraveling the intricate layers of a prophet of sound mind and years of discretion, deliberately and voluntarily turning away from the God ordained path and setting forth on a transformative journey of repentance and restoration within the sacred story.

The subtleties of spiritual suicide often elude statistical reports and societal discourse. Unlike more visible forms of self-destruction, this silent battle occurs within the lives of individuals who are part of a faith community, casting a shadow on the very hearts that should find sanctuary in the divine call. It is within this sacred space that our journey begins—a journey of introspection, understanding, repentance, and restoration.

As we delve into the chronical of Jonah, we discover a profound allegory that mirrors the struggles within our own faith community. The story not only reveals the manifestations and consequences of spiritual suicide but also illuminates the path to redemption. Jonah's journey becomes a guiding light, offering insights into the complexities of spiritual crisis and the transformative power of divine grace.

This exploration is not an ordinary recounting of a biblical story but an invitation to navigate sacred waters. With a faith-based audience in mind, we embark on a thoughtful examination of the intersections between faith, human frailty, and the persistent call to redemption. Join us in this pilgrimage of understanding and restoration as we seek to unravel the layers of spiritual suicide and, in doing so, rediscover the grace that can mend even the deepest wounds of the soul./

Navigating Spiritual Suicide: Crafting a Defining Framework

In the unfolding pages, we embark on an exploration of a profound concept — Spiritual Suicide. To navigate this complex terrain, let's first establish a shared understanding:

The term *'Spiritual'* is intricately woven with matters of the divine, intimately relating to God and sacred realms. It encompasses the essence of one's connection with the heavenly Father, reflecting the profound and transformative nature of a life lived in communion with spiritual principles.

On the other hand, 'Suicide' represents the intentional and voluntary act of taking one's own life. This act, executed by an individual of sound mind and years of discretion, delves beyond the physical realm, becoming a grave and weighty matter that transcends into the intricacies of the spiritual.

Together, the concept of 'Spiritual Suicide' encompasses a conscious and voluntary act by an individual of sound mind and years of discretion, involving the deliberate turning away from the divine path. This conscious act jeopardizes one's spiritual well-being, resonating in the choices we make, the priorities we set, and the alignment of our lives with the sacred principles that guide our existence.

As we embark on this journey through narratives and reflections, let this definition be our guiding light, illuminating the shadows of spiritual struggles that many of us encounter in the complex tapestry of our lives.

Chapter 1:
Navigating Spiritual Struggles

"The word of the Lord came to Jonah son of Amittai: 2 "Go to the great city of Nineveh and preach against it, because its wickedness has come up before me."3 But Jonah ran away from the Lord and headed for Tarshish. He went down to Joppa, where he found a ship bound for that port. After paying the fare, he went aboard and sailed for Tarshish to flee from the Lord.4 Then the Lord sent a great wind on the sea, and such a violent storm arose that the ship threatened to break up". Jonah 1:1-4 NIV

The Book of Jonah unfolds with the divine command echoing in the heart of the reluctant prophet, Jonah, son of Amittai. The directive is crystal clear: "Go to the great city of Nineveh and preach against it because its wickedness has come up before me." However, Jonah, in an act of voluntary defiance, chooses to sail in the opposite direction, abandoning his divine assignment.

This disobedience, a manifestation of spiritual suicide, not only jeopardizes Jonah's life but also places the lives of those sharing his journey at imminent risk. As we navigate Jonah's descent into spiritual suicide, let us reflect on the profound repercussions of disobedience within the sacred narrative.

The Narrative of Jonah

The account of Jonah serves as a reflective mirror, exposing the innate human tendency to resist Godly guidance. Jonah's disobedience is not an isolated incident; it encapsulates a broader pattern within the human experience.

Delving deeper into the psychology of defiance, we'll explore the motivations and rationalizations that lead individuals to willingly reject God's calling. Through this exploration, our goal is to cultivate a deep understanding of the intricate dynamics between human agency and divine purpose.

Modern Struggles: Following the Inner Call Amidst External Pressures

In a world where external expectations and societal norms exert considerable influence, the call to authenticity often clashes with the pressures to conform, especially within the Christian faith community. The story of Jonah resonates in contemporary struggles, mirroring situations where Christians grapple with staying true to their inner callings amidst external pressures.

Career Choices:

Consider the professional arena, where social expectations often dictate the trajectory of one's career. Many Christian individuals find themselves on paths that promise financial stability or social approval but deviate from their true passions and God-given talents.

The pressure to conform to established norms can lead to a subtle manifestation of deliberate and voluntary turning away from the sacred path, as Christians compromise their authentic selves and divine calling for the sake of social validation.

Relationships:

The realm of relationships is not immune to these struggles. Social expectations regarding partnerships, friendships, and family dynamics can create a conflict between Christian values and external pressures.

Christians may find themselves in compromising relationships that do not align with their spiritual or emotional well-being, succumbing to worldly expectations at the expense of their inner callings.

Personal Identity:

On a broader scale, the pressure to conform can influence personal identity. Society often imposes predefined roles and expectations based on gender, culture, or other social constructs.

The struggle to align personal identity with Christian values and biblical principles can lead to a sense of spiritual disconnection, as Christians navigate the delicate balance between self-discovery and societal conformity.

Reflection Moment:

As you delve into the modern struggles presented in this chapter, reflect on your own life as a Christian.

Are there areas where external pressures have nudged you away from your inner calling as guided by Christian principles?

How have societal expectations influenced your career choices, relationships, or personal identity within the context of your Christian faith?

In recognizing these subtle manifestations of spiritual suicide, you embark on a journey of self-discovery and introspection, seeking alignment with the divine plan.

The chronical of Jonah, intertwined with these modern struggles within the Christian faith community, serves as a guidepost, urging Christians to confront and rectify subtle rebellions against their inner callings.

Just as Jonah's disobedience carried profound consequences, the modern manifestations of spiritual suicide underscore the importance of aligning personal choices with Godly intent in the complex dance between social pressures, personal convictions, and the divine call that beckons within.

Anecdote:

In the parenting, or first ministry, season of my ministerial journey, I wrestled with a significant decision: whether to pursue a prestigious career outside the home, even though it conflicted with my true passion, traditional Christian values, and my tradition's emphasis on being a stay-at-home mother and wife.

The external pressures to conform were intense, tempting me to prioritize societal approval over the vital calling of this season. Eventually, I resisted succumbing to social expectations and chose to enter the workforce when my children reached elementary school age.

Conclusion:

As we conclude our exploration into Jonah's Descent into Spiritual Suicide, the echoes of deliberate defiance and the resonance of consequences linger in the air. Jonah's biblical story stands not just as a historical account but as a poignant reflection of our shared human inclination to resist spiritual guidance.

Through the complex layers of spiritual crisis unveiled in this chapter, we are invited to introspect on our own journeys. The struggle between personal choices and divine intent, mirrored in Jonah's disobedience, is a universal theme that transcends time.

In the modern struggles presented, we find echoes of Jonah's reluctance within our own faith community—struggles that manifest in career choices, relationships, and personal identity. The call to authenticity within the Christian tapestry often contends with external pressures, leading to subtle manifestations of spiritual suicide.

As we reflect on the narratives shared and embark on this pilgrimage of understanding, may we find resonance in our own stories and be inspired to align our choices with the divine calling, recognizing that the journey of redemption begins with acknowledging the echoes of Jonah within ourselves

Chapter 2:
Navigating the Tempest of Spiritual Turmoil

"All the sailors were afraid, and each cried out to his own god. And they threw the cargo into the sea to lighten the ship. But Jonah had gone below deck, where he lay down and fell into a deep sleep. 6 The captain went to him and said, "How can you sleep? Get up and call on your god! Maybe he will take notice of us so that we will not perish."7 Then the sailors said to each other, "Come, let us cast lots to find out who is responsible for this calamity." They cast lots and the lot fell on Jonah. 8 So they asked him, "Tell us, who is responsible for making all this trouble for us? What kind of work do you do? Where do you come from? What is your country? From what people are you?"9 He answered, "I am a Hebrew and I worship the Lord, the God of heaven, who made the sea and the dry land."10 This terrified them, and they asked, "What have you done?" (They knew he was running away from the Lord, because he had already told them so.) "Jonah 1: 5-10 (NIV)

As we plunge deeper into the realms of spiritual struggle, our vessel confronts turbulent waters, mirroring the internal storms faced by those ensnared in disobedience. Jonah 1:5-10 unveils a tempest upon the sea, a direct consequence of Jonah's defiance. This chapter aims to unearth the profound symbolism within the tempest, peeling back the layers of spiritual turmoil that besiege individuals when they deviate from their divine calling.

Symbolism of the Tempest:

Jonah's story presents the tempest as a potent metaphor for the internal chaos that ensues when we resist divine guidance. It signifies the far-reaching repercussions of disobedience, affecting not only the individual in defiance but also resonating through the lives of those in their proximity. Take a moment to reflect on the storms in your own life—instances where disobedience led to chaos, impacting not only yourself but also those around you.

In Jonah's story, the tempest jeopardizes not only Jonah's life but also the lives of the sailors on the ship. This collateral damage underscores the communal aspect of deliberate and voluntary turning away from the divine call. When we deviate from the path set by divine guidance, the consequences ripple outward, touching our relationships, communities, and even the broader body of believers. Consider the interconnectedness of our spiritual journeys and how our personal choices resonate beyond ourselves.

The Communal Impact of Disobedience:

The narrative in Jonah highlights the interconnectedness of our spiritual journeys. Jonah's disobedience doesn't occur in isolation; it reverberates through the lives of those sharing the voyage. The tempest becomes a communal crisis, emphasizing that spiritual suicide isn't a solitary act but one that affects the fabric of our communities. This chapter encourages us to consider the collateral damage our actions can inflict on those around us when we deliberately turn away from Godly guidance.

Cry for Divine Intervention:

Within the tempest's fury, the sailors cry out to their gods for salvation—a universal response to crisis, seeking a higher power for deliverance. In the midst of our spiritual turmoil, do we turn to God or rely on our own strength? This chapter extends an invitation for introspection, encouraging a deeper reliance on heavenly intervention during life's storms.

The Inner Storms of Our Lives:

As we delve into the symbolism of the tempest, take a moment to reflect on the inner storms you've encountered. These storms may manifest as personal struggles, doubts, or moments of disobedience. The tempest in Jonah's story prompts us to examine how we navigate our own internal chaos, whether by seeking Godly guidance or relying on our own understanding.

The Universality of Spiritual Tempests:

The tempest in Jonah's spiritual account transcends its historical context, resonating with the universal human experience. We all face storms—internal conflicts, doubts, or moments of disobedience—that threaten to engulf us. This chapter invites us to recognize the universality of these tempests and encourages a collective introspection into how we weather these storms individually and as a community.

Reflection Moment:

Pause and reflect on a tempestuous period in your life, possibly ignited by disobedience or deviation from spiritual guidance.

How did you navigate the storm?

To what gods did you turn for salvation?

Consider the lasting impact on those around you. As we explore Jonah's tempest, let it serve as a mirror for our own journeys, prompting a reconsideration of our responses to the storms of spiritual turmoil.

Anecdote:

During a season of disobedience, when God called me to leave my position and relocate to another state, I confronted a tempest that loomed over every aspect of my life—threatening my material possessions, including income, house, boat, car, and real estate endeavors, as well as my sense of freedom. The chaos extended beyond my personal sphere, impacting relationships and my overall sense of purpose. It was within this turmoil that I discovered the transformative power of surrender.

Turning to God amid the storm, I witnessed the tempest gradually subsiding as I made the move to another state, opening the door to a redemption I desperately needed.

Conclusion:

Jonah's tempest serves as a cautionary tale, urging us to confront the storms of spiritual turmoil that threaten our vessels. Through introspection, we navigate the symbolism of the tempest, recognizing the collateral damage of disobedience, and embracing the cry for divine intervention. Join us in exploring the tumultuous seas of spiritual crisis, where the beacon of redemption shines even in the darkest waves, illuminating the path to restoration and grace.

Chapter 3:
Consequences of Avoiding God's Calling

"In the hideout of denial, I confront the consequences of seeking refuge from God's calling" CM

The exploration of spiritual suicide in everyday life is a vital journey into the depth of our choices, behaviors, and priorities. As we unveil the diverse manifestations of this phenomenon, the tapestry of our existence becomes intricately woven with threads of caution and opportunity. This chapter serves as a mirror, reflecting not only the potential pitfalls but also the transformative power of awareness and authenticity.

In this space of introspection, we confront the consequences of avoiding divine calling, shedding light on the challenges inherent in seeking refuge from our spiritual responsibilities. Let us delve into the intricacies of this journey, recognizing that each choice carries profound implications for our spiritual well-being.

Exploring Potential Pitfalls:

Let's explore some potential pitfalls associated with spiritual suicide in everyday life:

Materialism Over Spiritual Well-being:

Pitfall: Constantly prioritizing material success and wealth at the expense of spiritual health.

Consequence: A sense of emptiness, spiritual disconnection, and a skewed perspective on life's purpose.

Work-Life Imbalance:

Pitfall: Neglecting the importance of rest, personal reflection, and spiritual practices due to an excessive focus on career and professional achievements.

Consequence: Burnout, strained relationships, and a diminished sense of spiritual fulfillment.

Superficial Relationships:

Pitfall: Engaging in relationships primarily for social or material gain rather than cultivating meaningful, spiritually enriching connections.

Consequence: Loneliness, a lack of emotional support, and a shallow understanding of interpersonal bonds.

Neglecting Spiritual Responsibilities:

Pitfall: Ignoring or avoiding spiritual duties and responsibilities, such as acts of kindness, charity, or participation in community worship.

Consequence: A sense of spiritual stagnation, missed opportunities for personal growth, and strained connections within the faith community.

Conforming to Societal Expectations:

Pitfall: Succumbing to societal pressures and expectations at the cost of my true spiritual calling.

Consequence: A feeling of inner conflict, a sense of unfulfillment, and a disconnection from my authentic spiritual path .

Unhealthy Lifestyle Choices:

Pitfall: Indulging in habits or behaviors that harm physical and mental well-being, neglecting the understanding that the body is a sacred vessel.

Consequence: Detrimental effects on overall health, hindrance to spiritual growth, and a diminished capacity to fulfill my purpose.

Spiritual Complacency:

Pitfall: Settling into a state of complacency, where there's a lack of active engagement with spiritual practices and a diminishing desire for personal growth.

Consequence: Stagnation in spiritual development, a weakened connection with our Heavenly Father and a diminished ability to navigate life's challenges.

These pitfalls are like subtle traps that can hinder my spiritual journey. Recognizing and addressing these challenges is a crucial step toward a more authentic and fulfilling spiritual life. Recognizing spiritual suicide is akin to navigating a labyrinth of decisions, each contributing to the fabric of my spiritual journey.

The hideouts of denial, whether in work, relationships, or personal pursuits, demand my attention and introspection. The reflection moments provided in this chapter serve as lanterns, illuminating the paths I may have overlooked and inviting me to confront the consequences of seeking refuge from God's calling.

Reflection Moment:

As we navigate the labyrinth of everyday decisions, ponder upon the subtle pitfalls that can lead to spiritual suicide. Reflect on own choices, behaviors, and priorities.

Where do you find your treasures, and how does it align with your spiritual well-being?

Consider the interconnectedness of your actions and their impact on your spiritual journey

Anecdote:

I recall a time in my life when the pursuit of success became an overwhelming priority. The more I achieved – a senior management position with a generous salary, a spacious 5-bedroom, 4-bath home in a gated resort community, a new car, and a boat – the more I felt a growing void within.

It took a moment of introspection and a deliberate shift in priorities to realize that true wealth lies not just in worldly accomplishments but in the richness of a spiritually aligned life. Confronting this pitfall became a transformative journey toward a more fulfilling existence.

Conclusion:

In concluding this chapter, we're presented with a reflection on the intricate interplay between choices and consequences in our spiritual journey. Rather than condemnations, the pitfalls uncovered serve as invitations to self-awareness and authenticity.

As we step out of the labyrinth, let us carry the lanterns of reflection, for in recognizing the shadows, we empower ourselves to walk in the transformative light of awareness and authenticity. Our journey continues, and with each step, we unravel the tapestry of our spiritual existence together.

Chapter 4:
Navigating Personal and Divine Realities

The chapter unfolds as an intimate exploration of my emotions, conflicts, and eventual breakthrough. Through the revelation of personal anecdotes, I unveil the vulnerability inherent in the journey through spiritual suicide. Building upon these challenges, special emphasis is given to the nuanced process of reconciling personal experiences with God's mandates.

The narrative expands to provide a raw and authentic glimpse into the intricate complexities of spiritual battles within the realm of ministry. This serves as a powerful demonstration that even those deeply immersed in service can grapple with their own spiritual warfare. In this pivotal chapter, we transition from the broader perspective of spiritual suicide to a deeply personal exploration of my own

Despite dedicating over 25 years to leadership in ministry within congregations and the marketplace—shepherding individuals towards Christ, facilitating healing, and deliverance—a significant shift occurs when confronted with God's call to minister marriage reconciliation and restoration to others, a prayer He had not manifested in my own life. This unexpected calling becomes the crucible for a profound struggle with obedience, creating a clash between my personal experiences and

God's command. This vividly illustrates the internal turmoil that leads to deliberate and voluntary turning away from God's calling.

In the busy season of my life, the demands from family responsibilities, ministry service, and engagement in the marketplace created internal conflict. The pressure to excel in all three areas led to moments of doubt and spiritual questioning. I found myself grappling with societal norms that prioritize living to work, while also feeling the call to remain faithful to my divine purpose—shepherding members in church through ministry leadership, providing pastoral care in my community, and serving my family. This internal conflict became a catalyst for growth, a transformative process that reshaped my understanding of spiritual battles within the complexities of modern life.

Exploring Modern Challenges:

The chapter unfolds as an intimate exploration of my emotions, conflicts, and eventual breakthrough. Through the revelation of personal anecdotes, I unveil the vulnerability inherent in the journey through spiritual suicide. Special emphasis is given to the nuanced process of reconciling personal experiences with God's mandates. The narrative expands to provide a raw and authentic glimpse into the intricate complexities of spiritual battles within the realm of ministry. It serves as a powerful demonstration that even those deeply immersed in service can grapple with their own spiritual challenge.

Examples of Spiritual Battles in Ministry

Obedience Struggles:

Wrestling with the call to deliver a challenging message: The internal conflict when faced with delivering a sermon or message that challenges congregants to confront uncomfortable truths, knowing it may lead to resistance or criticism.

Personal vs. Divine Experience:

Balancing personal experiences with Godly mandates: The tension between personal struggles, doubts, or questioning of faith, and the responsibility to exemplify unwavering faith and trust in God's guidance.

Burnout and Self-Care:

Experiencing burnout and the need for self-care: Candidly sharing moments of exhaustion, the weight of pastoral responsibilities, and the struggle to find a healthy balance between serving others and maintaining personal well-being.

Navigating Criticism:

Confronting criticism and doubts within the congregation: Addressing instances where personal decisions or actions are met with skepticism or opposition within the church community, and the emotional toll it takes on the minister.

Technology and Ministry:

Impact of modern challenges on spiritual life: Exploring the influence of technology, social media, and the fast-paced nature of modern life on maintaining a spiritually grounded existence, and the challenges of adapting ministry to these changes

Community Conflicts:

Resolving conflicts within the church community: Sharing experiences of mediating conflicts, whether interpersonal or related to differing perspectives on faith, and the internal struggle to maintain unity and harmony.

Mental Health Stigma:

Confronting mental health challenges: Opening up about personal struggles with anxiety, depression, or other mental health issues, and the stigma attached to seeking help within faith communities

Navigating Modern Challenges:

My leadership roles and experiences within ministry become integral to this exploration. I faced contemporary challenges that were more centered around personal relationships and a longing for job security in secular roles, all while aligning with God's purpose for my life.

While acknowledging that the challenges within the socializing landscape and professional aspirations may differ from more contemporary concerns, it's important to recognize that each individual struggle with their own unique battles.

Reflection Moment:

In navigating my personal journey through the challenges of deliberate and voluntary turning away from God's divine path, parallels emerge with the detailed struggles of individuals in biblical narratives. The conflicts faced aren't unique to a few ancient figures; they resonate across time and circumstances.

As you delve into these reflections, consider your own spiritual struggles.

What aspects of your journey align with the challenges faced by those navigating the complexities of faith and worldly demands?

How can these shared chronicles inspire a deeper introspection into your own choices, guiding you toward a path of renewal and alignment with ordained purpose?

Anecdote:

In the midst of my own errors, as I avoided God's call during my divorce season, I entered into a courtship after several years of abstaining, eventually becoming intimately involved. The relationship held promise with shared interests, and everything appeared perfect until the resounding echo of God's call disrupted the apparent harmony.

Despite the allure of an amazing person offering an affluent lifestyle, I was met with an unexpected outpouring of God's compassion when I made the challenging choice to obey Him. In that moment, His grace became a guiding light, revealing a path I had not anticipate.

Conclusion:

As we conclude this chapter, the journey through my personal struggle with spiritual suicide reveals the delicate dance between earthly challenges and God's calling. The intertwining threads of my leadership roles, ministry experiences, and the confrontation of modern-day pressures serve as a testament to the universality of the spiritual battle. This intimate exploration, rooted in vulnerability, lays bare the complexities inherent in reconciling personal experiences with the higher calling

Transformative Invitation:

Through the lens of my journey, I extend an invitation to you, dear reader, to embark on your own introspective expedition. Recognize that the path to spiritual wholeness often involves navigating the complex dance between personal experiences and divine calling. As we move forward, let this chapter serve as a guidepost, urging you to confront your own spiritual struggles with honesty and courage.

In the sacred space of vulnerability, there lies a catalyst for transformation. Our shared journey becomes a mirror, reflecting not just the challenges but also the immense potential for growth and alignment with God's purpose. So, with this invitation, we move forward, united in our pursuit of spiritual authenticity and redemption.

Chapter 5:

Storms of Distress and God's Awakening

Embarking on a seven-year separation, the author traverses' storms of distress, losing material possessions along the way. The comfort of the "Hideout" transforms into a precarious refuge as the storms intensify, introspection. In this chapter, we delve into the author's journey through adversity, recognizing that storms and separation from God serve as catalysts for seeking His face. We unravel the profound lesson that God orchestrates events, even storms, to accomplish His purpose.

Metaphorical Landscape of Transformation:

The storms become a metaphorical landscape of transformation and awakening. By unpacking the author's seven-year separation, readers gain insights into the dynamics of divine intervention during times of distress. The exploration extends to include psychological and theological perspectives on the role of adversity in spiritual growth.

PYCHOLOGICAL PERSPECTIVE

Resilience and Post-Traumatic Growth:

Psychological research suggests that individuals can develop resilience in the face of adversity. Experiencing and overcoming challenges can lead to post-traumatic growth, where individuals emerge stronger, more resilient, and with a deeper sense of meaning and purpose.

James 1:2-4 (ESV): "Count it all joy, my brothers, when you meet trials of various kinds, for you know that the testing of your faith produces steadfastness. And let steadfastness have its full effect, that you may be perfect and complete, lacking in nothing."

Identity Development:

Adversity often prompts individuals to reevaluate their values, priorities, and sense of identity. It can be a catalyst for personal growth, self-discovery, and a more profound understanding of one's own capabilities.

Romans 12:2 (NIV): "Do not conform to the pattern of this world but be transformed by the renewing of your mind. Then you will be able to test and approve what God's will is—his good, pleasing and perfect will."

Cognitive Appraisal:

The way individuals perceive and appraise adversity can influence its impact. Cognitive theories emphasize that one's thoughts and interpretations of challenging situations play a crucial role in determining the emotional and spiritual consequences.

Philippians 4:8 (NIV): "Finally, brothers and sisters, whatever is true, whatever is noble, whatever is right, whatever is pure, whatever is lovely, whatever is admirable—if anything is excellent or praiseworthy—think about such things."

THEOLOGICAL PERSPECTIVE

Purification and Refinement:

Theological perspectives often view adversity as a means of purification and refinement. Just as fire refines precious metals, challenges can refine and purify the spirit, removing impurities and drawing individuals closer to God.

Malachi 3:3 (NIV): "He will sit as a refiner and purifier of silver; he will purify the Levites and refine them like gold and silver. Then the Lord will have men who will bring offerings in righteousness."

Testing and Faith Development:

Adversity is seen as a test of faith in many theological traditions. Enduring trials can strengthen faith, deepen trust in God's providence, and foster a more intimate relationship with the divine.

1 Peter 1:7 (ESV): "So that the tested genuineness of your faith—more precious than gold that perishes though it is tested by fire—may be found to result in praise and glory and honor at the revelation of Jesus Christ."

Redemptive Suffering:

Some theological perspectives emphasize the concept of redemptive suffering, suggesting that challenges and suffering, when endured with faith, can contribute to the redemptive work of God in the world.

Colossians 1:24 (NIV): "Now I rejoice in what I am suffering for you, and I fill up in my flesh what is still lacking in regard to Christ's afflictions, for the sake of his body, which is the church."

Transformation and Spiritual Maturity:

Adversity is viewed as a transformative process that leads to spiritual maturity. The challenges faced are seen as opportunities for individuals to align themselves more closely with God's divine purpose.

2 Corinthians 3:18 (NIV): "And we all, who with unveiled faces contemplate the Lord's glory, are being transformed into his image with ever-increasing glory, which comes from the Lord, who is the Spirit."

Compassion and Empathy:

Experiencing adversity can cultivate compassion and empathy for others who are suffering. The theological notion of walking in the footsteps of Christ's suffering is often associated with the development of compassion.

2 Corinthians 1:3-4 (NIV): "Praise be to the God and Father of our Lord Jesus Christ, the Father of compassion and the God of all comfort, who comforts us in all our troubles, so that we can comfort those in any trouble with the comfort we ourselves receive from God."

Combining these psychological and theological perspectives with scripture references provides a comprehensive understanding of how adversity can contribute to spiritual growth, resilience, and a deeper connection with our Heavenly Father.

Reflection Moment:

In this chapter, we've explored how the storms of life, both personal and global, parallel Jonah's tumultuous journey. Consider the storms you've weathered in your own life — the challenges, uncertainties, and moments of distress. How did these storms shape your spiritual landscape? Were there awakenings amidst the turbulence? Reflect on the profound realization that, like Jonah, the storms we face can be transformative, prompting us to reevaluate our priorities and seek a deeper connection with God.

Anecdote:

I weathered many storms of distress that stripped away the purposeless layers of my life — the senior management position, the car, the sale of my house, and the boat I rarely enjoyed due to work demands. These losses included meaningful relationships, adding another layer to the spiritual crisis, a manifestation of spiritual suicide. However, as I confronted the storm with faith, repentance, and resilience, I discovered the Holy Spirit's transformative and purifying power, washing away distractions and revealing a deeper connection with God. Rectifying the subtle manifestations of spiritual suicide involved embracing the storms, including the loss of meaningful relationships, as opportunities for profound awakening.

Conclusion:

In the storms of distress and awakening, my family and I have navigated the tumultuous terrain of my seven-year separation, discovering profound lessons in the midst of adversity. As we conclude this chapter, let the echoes of the storms, including the heartbreaking loss of meaningful relationships, resonate within you, recognizing that challenges, though formidable, are gateways to transformation.

The storms faced, both personal and collective, are not mere hindrances; they are opportunities for divine awakening and redirection. Embrace the storms, along with the profound loss of meaningful relationships, as companions in your journey, knowing that, like Jonah, you can find solace and inspiration even in the tempests of life. As we transition to the next chapter, may the wisdom gained in the storms, including the understanding of loss, illuminate your path toward deeper connection and purpose.

Chapter 6:
God's Compassion and Second Chances.

In the depth of the belly of the whale, Jonah experiences an extraordinary outpouring of God's compassion, marking the beginning of a profound second chance. This chapter delves into the narrative of Jonah, drawing parallels between his encounter with divine grace and our own opportunities for redemption.

As we explore Jonah's story alongside relevant scripture references, we reflect on the boundless nature of God's mercy and the transformative power embedded in the theme of divine compassion and second chances.

The Depths of God's Compassion:

Jonah's Desperate Prayer Jonah 2:1-10 (NIV) captures Jonah's prayer from the belly of the whale, portraying a moment of distress, calling out to God, and experiencing God's attentive response. This prayer becomes a poignant reminder that, even in the depths of our mistakes, God's compassion is ready to meet us.

God's Reprieve for Nineveh

Turning our gaze to Jonah 3:10 (NIV), we witness the transformative power of divine compassion in response to Nineveh's repentance. The verse reveals God's decision to relent from the planned disaster upon witnessing the genuine turn from evil by the people of Nineveh. As we reflect on these scriptures, we are prompted to explore moments in our lives where divine compassion and second chances have intersected with our own stories.

Consider times when, like Jonah, you found yourself in the depths, calling out for mercy, and experienced an unexpected outpouring of God's compassion. Additionally, ponder instances where, through repentance and transformation, you witnessed the relenting of divine judgment in your life.

This section serves as a tapestry woven with threads of grace, inviting readers to recognize the transformative power of divine compassion in their own lives. Through shared reflections and stories of resilience, we illuminate the path to renewal, encouraging readers to embrace the boundless mercy that awaits those who choose the journey of repentance and spiritual rebirth.

Reflection Moment:

As we contemplate God's compassion and the theme of second chances, let's draw parallels to our own lives. Recall moments of God's intervention, instances where grace abounded in the face of our spiritual shortcomings. Consider your personal redemption narratives—times when, like Jonah, you found yourself in the depths, calling out for mercy, and experienced an unexpected outpouring of God's compassion.

Reflect on instances where, through repentance and transformation, you witnessed the relenting of God's judgment in your life. In exploring God's compassion and the gift of second chances, we unveil a story of hope and redemption that transcends personal experiences.

This chapter becomes a tapestry woven with threads of grace, inviting readers to recognize the transformative power of God's compassion in their own lives. Through shared reflections and stories of resilience, we illuminate the path to renewal, encouraging readers to embrace the boundless mercy that awaits those who choose the journey of repentance and spiritual rebirth.

Anecdote:

Actively engaged in my church community, I faced persistent inquiries from the pastor, questioning my evasion of God's call. Each Sunday brought a renewed emphasis, reminding me that the door to God's purpose might one day close, haunting me with the specter of 'too late.'

Navigating this unforeseen second chance became a turbulent journey of emotions, grappling with guilt for sidestepping my calling and the necessity of walking away from a meaningful relationship. During this emotional whirlwind, I felt profound relief at the prospect of a second chance and deep gratitude for the pastor's unwavering persistence. The environment was charged with uncertainty, and the weight of my choices hung palpably in the atmosphere.

Accepting this grace with humility marked the beginning of a deliberate journey of spiritual renewal. Beyond acknowledging my spiritual neglect, I embarked on practical steps to align with

God's divine call. The pages of God's word unfolded before me as a sacred guide to understanding His purpose.

Fasting became a soulful commitment, a tangible expression of my hunger for spiritual nourishment. Each prayer became a heartfelt conversation, a lifeline connecting me to God. Active participation in the church community reinforced my sense of belonging in God's family.

Through these dedicated practices, I discovered the profound impact of God's compassion on my life. The words on the pages became a source of wisdom and comfort, guiding me through the labyrinth of doubts. Fasting became a purifying journey, cleansing my spirit and fostering resilience. Prayer became a conduit for God's guidance, a reassuring presence in moments of uncertainty. Active participation in the church community became a supportive network, reminding me that I was not alone in this transformative journey.

This anecdote, illustrating the complex interplay of emotions and actions, stands as a testament to the transformative power of God's compassion. The atmosphere, once heavy with uncertainty, now resonates with a renewed sense of purpose. The weight of choices has transformed into the buoyancy of grace, lifting me towards spiritual renewal.

Conclusion:

As we conclude this chapter, the resounding truth echoes through the narrative of Jonah and my own journey—a truth that transcends time and personal experiences. It is the unwavering proclamation that God's compassion knows no bounds. In the depth of the whale's belly, Jonah experienced a divine outpouring of mercy, marking the genesis of a profound second chance.

This chapter, entwined with the threads of Jonah's prayer and the transformative power of God's compassion, extends an invitation to readers. It urges them to recognize the boundless nature of God's mercy, reminding that, regardless of the depths of their struggles or the weight of their mistakes, a second chance awaits.

The theme of God's compassion becomes a beacon of hope, inviting individuals to embark on a transformative journey of spiritual rebirth. The echoes of Jonah's prayer and the subsequent redemption of Nineveh reverberate in our reflections. We contemplate our own moments of distress, calling out for mercy, and the unexpected, overwhelming compassion that met us in those depths.

Through shared stories of resilience and redemption, we illuminate the path to renewal, encouraging readers to embrace the boundless mercy that stands ready for those who choose the transformative journey of repentance.

As we transition to the next chapter, let the recognition of God's compassion linger in your spirit. May this understanding become a source of hope and inspiration, empowering you to move forward with confidence in God's unwavering love and the infinite possibilities of spiritual rebirth that grace awaits.

Chapter 7:
Answering God's Call

"In my distress, I called to the Lord, and he answered me. From deep in the realm of the dead, I called for help, and you listened to my cry." Jonah 2:2 (NIV)

Introduction:

In the midst of life's storms, we often find ourselves standing at the crossroads of God's guidance, mirroring Jonah's journey. This chapter invites you to explore the transformative path of answering God's call, aligning your steps with a higher purpose. Let's delve into the roadmap that unfolds in the echoes of Jonah's prayer, discovering practical steps for discernment and obedience.

Exploration of God's Calling

This chapter serves as a guiding light for readers navigating their divine calling. Join us on a journey that intertwines biblical principles and real-life examples, offering tools to confront spiritual battles and confidently answer the call toward repentance and restoration.

Practical Steps for Discerning and Answering God's Call:

Embarking on the path of answering God's call necessitates a willingness to discern His guidance and take intentional steps toward obedience. Here are practical steps, supported by relevant scriptures, to assist you on this transformative journey:

Cultivate a Spirit of Humility (James 4:10):

Approach the journey with humility, surrendering your plans and desires to allow God to lead.

Repent and Turn Away from Sin (Acts 3:19):

Examine your life, confess sins, and turn away from behaviors contrary to God's will, opening the door to divine refreshing and

Seek God in Prayer and Meditation

(Philippians 4:6-7):

Establish a consistent prayer life, seeking God's wisdom and guidance through meditation on His Word.

Align Decisions with God's Word

(Psalm 119:105):

Immerse yourself in Scripture, making God's Word the guiding light for decisions that align with His principles.

Seek Wise Counsel (Proverbs 15:22):

Surround yourself with wise and spiritually mature individuals, seeking godly insights and perspectives.

Observe Open and Closed Doors (Revelation 3:7):

Pay attention to opportunities and obstacles, trusting that God directs your path by opening and closing doors according to His plan.

Listen to the Holy Spirit (John 16:13):

Cultivate sensitivity to the Holy Spirit's leading, allowing it to guide decisions and prompt obedience.

Act in Faith, Trusting God's Providence. (Proverbs 3:5-6):

Step out in faith, trusting that God's providence will unfold as actions align with His will.

Remember, discerning and answering God's call is an ongoing journey. Be patient, persistent, and attentive to His leading, knowing that He is faithful to guide those who seek Him.

In the Current Landscape:

In today's complex landscape, individuals may be navigating significant decisions related to personal and professional lives. This chapter offers insights into the importance of discernment and obedience in the face of uncertainty, resonating with those making life-altering choices.

Reflection Moment:

As we conclude this chapter, take a moment to reflect on your journey of discernment and obedience. Have there been calls from God that you've hesitated to answer? Consider the transformative impact of answering God's call on your life and those around you. This moment of reflection is an opportunity to discern the calls lingering in your heart and reaffirm your commitment to answer with a resounding "yes.

Anecdote:

Within the pages of this book, testimonies serve as mirrors reflecting universal themes of doubt, repentance, restoration, and the transformative power of divine intervention. May my journey, akin to Jonah's, inspire you to confront your spiritual battles, embrace the path of renewal, and answer the call that beckons you toward a life of purpose and obedience.

Conclusion:

As we reach the culmination of this transformative journey, the importance of obedience and submission emerges as a resounding theme. Through the trials of Jonah and the author's personal testimony, we witness the transformative power of God's intervention. The journey from spiritual suicide to redemption is not merely a narrative; it extends an invitation for readers to confront their struggles, embrace God's grace, and embark on a transformative journey of renewal.

May the narratives within these pages serve as a reflective mirror, revealing universal themes of doubt, repentance, restoration, and the profound transformation achievable through divine intervention. Let the journey, much like Jonah's, inspire you to confront your spiritual battles, embrace the path of renewal, and answer the call that beckons you toward a life of purpose and obedience.

As you navigate the uncharted territories of your divine calling, may this chapter stand as a guiding light, offering practical wisdom and spiritual insights to support you on your journey of discernment and obedience. Remember, the transformative power of answering God's call is universal. In this concluding moment, embrace the calls that linger in your heart, reaffirm your commitment, and answer with a resounding 'yes.'"

Chapter 8:
The Impact of Obedience

———

"Then the word of the Lord came to Jonah a second time: 'Go to the great city of Nineveh and proclaim to it the message I give you.' Jonah obeyed the word of the Lord and went to Nineveh" (Jonah 3:1-3, NIV).

In this chapter, we delve into the remarkable account of Jonah's second commission to go to Nineveh. God, in His infinite mercy, gives Jonah another chance to fulfill His command. As we explore this biblical narrative, we will unravel the profound impact of obedience not just on the obedient individual but also on a larger scale, emphasizing the interconnectedness of our actions and the greater good they can bring.

Exploring Jonah's Second Commission:

Turning our attention to Jonah 3, we encounter God's persistent call for Jonah to go to Nineveh. Despite Jonah's initial disobedience and attempted escape, God's plan for Nineveh's salvation remains steadfast. Jonah, having experienced the consequences of disobedience, now responds in obedience, going to the great city and proclaiming the message of repentance.

As Jonah faced the divine call once more, what internal conflicts churned within him? How did he grapple with the weight of obedience after the repercussions of his initial disobedience? These aspects delve into the emotional and mental landscape of Jonah's journey.

Nineveh's Repentance:

Jonah's obedience triggers a miraculous chain of events. The people of Nineveh, from the greatest to the least, respond to Jonah's message. They declare a fast, put on sackcloth, and turn from their evil ways. Witnessing their genuine repentance, God relents from the disaster He had planned, showcasing the transformative power of obedience not only on an individual level but on an entire city.

"The Ninevites believed God. A fast was proclaimed, and all of them, from the greatest to the least, put on sackcloth. When Jonah's warning reached the king of Nineveh, he rose from his throne, took off his royal robes, covered himself with sackcloth and sat down in the dust... When God saw what they did and how they turned from their evil ways, he relented and did not bring on them the destruction he had threatened" (Jonah 3:5-10, NIV).

Exploring the Rewards of Obedience:

Drawing parallels from Jonah's experience, we recognize that obedience goes beyond individual transformation. The repentance of Nineveh brings about blessings and spared calamity for an entire nation. This highlights the profound impact that one person's obedience can have on a collective level, showcasing the interconnectedness of our actions.

Reflecting on my own journey, I've witnessed the personal rewards of obedience, from divine favor to spiritual fulfillment. These aspects can be mirrored in your life as well. How has obedience opened doors to God's favor and blessings for you?

Personal Rewards of Obedience:

God's Favor and Blessings (Proverbs 16:20): "Whoever gives heed to instruction prospers and blessed is the one who trusts in the Lord." Obedience opens the door to God's favor and blessings. Explore how aligning with God's will brings about prosperity in various aspects of life.

Spiritual Fulfillment (John 4:34): "My food," said Jesus, "is to do the will of him who sent me and to finish his work." Reflect on how obedience leads to a profound sense of purpose and spiritual fulfillment. Discover the joy that comes from doing God's work.

Impact on Others (Matthew 5:16): "In the same way, let your light shine before others, that they may see your good deeds and glorify your Father in heaven." Explore how obedience becomes a testimony that influences and inspires those around you. Your actions can lead others to glorify God.

Protection and Guidance (Psalm 32:8): "I will instruct you and teach you in the way you should go; I will counsel you with my loving eye on you." Delve into the assurance of God's guidance and protection that accompanies obedience. Trusting in His leading provides a sense of security.

Fulfillment of God's Purposes (Jeremiah 29:11): "'For I know the plans I have for you,' declares the Lord, 'plans to prosper you and not to harm you, plans to give you hope and a future.'" Jonah's obedience led to the fulfillment of God's purpose for Nineveh. Explore how your obedience aligns with God's greater plan for your life.

Benefits to Others for the Greater Good:

Obedience is not just a personal journey; it has the potential to create a ripple effect of blessings. As we explore the rewards of obedience, let's consider how Jonah's obedience not only averted disaster for Nineveh but also became a catalyst for the spiritual revival of an entire community.

"When God saw what they did and how they turned from their evil ways, he relented and did not bring on them the destruction he had threatened" (Jonah 3:10, NIV).

Reflection Moment:

As I reflect on some of these instances of obedience, I am humbled by the sophisticated tapestry woven by each act of faithfulness. The obedience to write, to share, and to adapt in challenging times has, in turn, impacted individuals, marriages, and students in ways I may never fully comprehend. It serves as a reminder that our acts of obedience, regardless of how small or seemingly insignificant, can set off a chain reaction of blessings beyond our understanding.

Consider your own moments of obedience. How have your acts of faithfulness, no matter how modest, contributed to the greater good? Reflect on the interconnected nature of obedience and the potential it holds to touch lives in ways we may never anticipate.

Anecdote:

In various seasons of my life, I've witnessed the profound impact of obedience on the greater good. One instance stands out as a testament to the interconnectedness of obedience and its far-reaching consequences. Reflecting on these moments reminds me of the incredible rewards that obedience can bring.

During my parenting seasons, confronting and resolving internal conflicts became transformative experiences. Amazingly, they led to the blessing of being present with my five children during their formative years. This journey taught me important virtues such as patience, unconditional love, kindness, empathy, consistency, self-control, and commitment. It underscored the significance of authenticity within the context of my Christian faith, reinforcing the idea that the God's plan often unfolds in ways that defy societal expectations.

From crafting and implementing the steps for 'Mending Hearts from Separation to Restoration,' facilitating the restoration of marriages, to writing an evangelistic play called 'The Devil is a

Liar'—this play profoundly stirred hearts and led individuals to reconsider their beliefs. Initiatives like starting a Step Ministry and launching 'A Willing to Wait,' advocating abstinence until marriage, further extended the reach and impact of my efforts.

Another significant moment arose when I was inspired to write the book 'The DREAM System: Discovering Your Life Purpose' in a mere 16 days. The urgency was fueled by my mother's diagnosis of stage 4 cancer; she desired a tangible copy before her passing. This act, born from obedience and love, became a source of comfort for her in her final days.

The impact extended to sharing this published work with graduating students, where the seeds of purpose were planted in young hearts. When my professional position faced elimination, I found myself revisiting the DREAM System. In this season of uncertainty, I revised the framework, crafted a complementary workbook, and embarked on the journey of writing this very book. The true impact of these endeavors may not be immediately evident, but I trust that it will be far-reaching and immeasurable, guided by the sacred hand of commencement.

Conclusion:

In closing, this chapter invites us to recognize that obedience is not merely a personal transaction with God; it is a catalyst for blessings that extend beyond our individual spheres. My journey, marked by obedience in various forms, serves as a testament to the transformative power that emanates when we align our steps with God's guidance.

May we embrace the truth that our acts of obedience, whether evident or concealed, have the potential to impact the greater good. The rewards of obedience are not confined to personal blessings; they echo in the lives of those around us, creating a life of Godly influence that surpasses our understanding. As we move forward, let us step into obedience with the anticipation of far-reaching consequences, trusting that God's plan unfolds in ways that go beyond our immediate comprehension.

Chapter 9:
Notable Disobedient Characters:

————

Welcome to the "Hall of Fame of Disobedience," a special exploration into the stories of notable biblical characters who, like Jonah, grappled with the challenges of obeying God's instructions. If Jonah's narrative didn't entirely resonate with your experiences, perhaps you'll find a reflection of your struggles in the journeys of these Hall of Fame members. Each character's disobedience brought about profound consequences, offering poignant lessons for us all.

————

Parallels with Jonah:

Adam: Disobeyed God's command not to eat from the tree of knowledge, leading to consequences (Genesis 3:17-19). Result: Expelled from the Garden of Eden and introduced to the toil of the land.

Sarah: Sought to fulfill God's promise in her own way, resulting in complications (Genesis 16:4-6). Result: Hagar and Ishmael's expulsion.

Moses: Struck the rock in disobedience, affecting his entry into the Promised Land (Numbers 20:12). Result: Unable to enter the Promised Land.

Samson: Revealed his source of strength, contrary to God's instructions, leading to his downfall (Judges 16:21-30). Result: Captured, blinded, and his final act of strength leading to his death.

Reflection Moment

As we journey through this chapter, let's take a deeply personal look at the lives of disobedient biblical figures. Their stories echo through the corridors of time, reminding us of our own struggles with obedience and faith.

Think about your own journey—are there moments where you've felt the tug of disobedience, ignoring God's voice for the allure of worldly desires or the comfort of familiarity?

Reflect on these instances with honesty and humility. How can the lessons learned from these biblical characters inform your own choices today?

Consider how embracing obedience can lead to a deeper connection with God and a more fulfilling spiritual journey

Anecdote:

There were many pivotal moments when I hesitated to answer profound calls from God. Fear and uncertainty gripped me, questioning my ability to fulfill the purpose laid out before me. Much like Adam, Sarah, Moses, and Samson, I grappled with the weight of my own doubts and insecurities. Yet, as I mustered the courage to answer, the journey that unfolded brought unimaginable blessings and a profound sense of fulfillment.

Rectifying the subtle manifestations of spiritual suicide involved stepping beyond the comfort of the known, answering the call with faith, and experiencing the transformative power of repentance and obedience.

Conclusion:

May this chapter stand as a guiding light, offering practical wisdom and spiritual insights to support you on your journey of discernment and obedience.

Remember, the transformative power of answering God's call is universal. In this concluding moment, embrace the calls that linger in your heart, reaffirm your commitment, and answer with a resounding 'yes.'

Closing Prayer:

Dear Heavenly Father,

In the sacred space of reflection, we come before You with hearts laid bare. You, who know the depths of our struggles, doubts, fears and moments of disobedience, we pray for Your mercy and compassion.

We thank You for the stories of Jonah, Adam, Sarah, Moses, and Samson, each woven into the tapestry of our understanding. Their journeys, marked by defiance, hesitation, and stumbling, resonate within the corridors of our own hearts.

As we close this chapter of exploration and introspection, we repent and ask for your forgiveness for our shortcomings and disobedience, surrendering them to Your never-ending love. We stand in awe of Your transformative power, the mercy that extends beyond our understanding, and the countless chances You generously provide.

May this prayer be a testament to our commitment to answer Your call, to confront our spiritual battles, and to embrace the journey of renewal. We acknowledge that repentance is not a one-time act but a continuous path, and we trust in Your guidance as we move forward.

In moments of doubt and fear, may Your Word be a lamp unto our feet, and a light unto our path. In times of adversity, may Your compassion be our comfort. As we navigate the complexities of life, may Your divine grace guide us toward obedience and alignment with Your sacred purpose.

We humbly ask for Your forgiveness of our sins and offer repentance, not just for ourselves but for all who embark on this transformative journey. May Your love, mercy, and grace abound, leading us from spiritual suicide to the shores of Godly repentance and restoration.

In Jesus Holy name, we pray.

Amen.

Closing Reflection:

As you turn the final pages of this transformative journey, remember that the narrative does not end here; it continues within the chapters of your own life. Each page turned is an invitation to embrace the unfolding story of your spiritual journey, marked by moments of doubt, uncertainty, and profound revelation. In the face of challenges, find courage to confront your inner struggles and uncertainties, knowing that within the depths of your being lies an unyielding strength waiting to be awakened.

Amidst the storms of life, draw upon the reservoir of resilience that resides within you, knowing that every trial is an opportunity for growth and self-discovery. As you navigate the twists and turns of your path, may you find solace in the unwavering guidance of a compassionate God, whose presence is a constant beacon of hope in the darkest of hours.

Remember, too, that second chances abound for those who are willing to heed the divine call. No matter how far you may have strayed or how insurmountable the obstacles may seem, the path to redemption is always open to those who seek it earnestly. Trust in the transformative power of God's grace to lead you towards repentance, renewal, and restoration.

As you close this chapter of introspection and embark on the next phase of your spiritual journey, carry with you the lessons learned, the wisdom gained, and the profound assurance that you are never alone. May the light of God's love illuminate your path, guiding you towards a deeper understanding of yourself and a closer communion with God

Appendix: Study Guide

Chapter 1: The Call of Repentance

- What are your initial thoughts on the concept of repentance?

- Can you relate to Jonah's reluctance in any aspects of your life?

- How do you recognize a call to repentance in your own journey?

Chapter 2: The Depths of Disobedience

- Reflect on a time when you faced the consequences of disobedience.

- How did Jonah's flight resonate with times when you tried to escape responsibility?

- In what ways can confronting disobedience lead to personal growth and healing?

Chapter 3: Confronting the Consequences of Avoiding God's Calling

- Which potential pitfalls of spiritual suicide do you find most relevant to your life?

- Share a personal reflection moment inspired by the chapter.

- How can awareness and authenticity contribute to overcoming the hideouts of denial?

Chapter 4: The Transformative Power of Repentance

- Explore the emotions conveyed in Jonah's prayer. How do they relate to your experiences?

- Share a personal healing journey from a time of repentance.

- How does repentance contribute to spiritual and emotional well-being?

Chapter 5: Navigating the Storms of Life

- Reflect on a personal encounter with a "storm" in your life.

- How can one find calm amidst chaos, drawing inspiration from Jonah's experience?

- Discuss the role of faith in navigating life's storms.

Chapter 6: From the Belly of the Whale to the Shore of Redemption

- Relate Jonah's deliverance to a time when you felt rescued from a challenging situation.

- How does embracing redemption impact one's outlook on life?

- Share personal insights into the transformative power of second chances.

Chapter 7: Obedience and Second Chances

- Explore your thoughts on second chances, drawing parallels from Jonah's narrative.

- How can obedience be a catalyst for personal transformation?

- Share personal experiences of second chances and their impact.

Chapter 8: The Impact of Obedience - Nineveh's Repentance

- Reflect on the interconnectedness of actions and their impact on a larger scale.

- How does Jonah's experience highlight the potential blessings of obedience?

- Share instances where personal obedience had a positive impact on others.

Chapter 9: Notable Disobedient Characters

- How can embracing obedience lead to a deeper connection with God and a more fulfilling spiritual journey?

- Are there moments where you've felt the tug of disobedience, ignoring God's voice for the allure of worldly desires or the comfort of familiarity?

- How can the lessons learned from these biblical characters inform your own choices today?

Conclusion

- What reflections do you carry from the entire journey of the book?

- How has your perspective on repentance and obedience evolved?

- What steps can you take to embrace a purposeful life based on the book's teachings?

About the Author

Introducing Dr. Carla McArthur – Your Expert Guide to a Purpose-Driven Life!

Dr. Carla McArthur, a seasoned Biblical Transformational Life Coach, is your dedicated partner in navigating the complexities of personal and professional life. Beyond traditional coaching, she offers a collaborative approach to foster a well-rounded, healthy, and purpose-driven lifestyle.

With over two decades of leadership experience in nonprofit and faith-based organizations, Dr. McArthur has honed her skills in counseling, coaching, and mentoring to bring about positive transformations in the lives of individuals. Her commitment to empowering women and youth extends beyond coaching, as she imparts practical wisdom drawn from real-life experiences.

Dr. McArthur's academic achievements include a Doctor of Ministry in Christian Counseling, a Master of Divinity specializing in the Psychology of Religion in Pastoral Counseling from the Interdenominational Theological Center, and studies in Nonprofit Management at Eastern University School of Professional Studies. Holding credentials as a Licensed and Ordained Minister, an NCCA Licensed Clinical Pastoral Counselor, a Certified Temperament Counselor, Certified Laughter Wellness Coach, and a Nationally Certified Entrepreneur Coach, she brings a comprehensive and well-rounded expertise to her coaching practice.

In addition to her professional pursuits, Dr. McArthur finds fulfillment in exploring museums, partaking in outdoor adventures, maintaining an active fitness routine, and immersing herself in the fine arts. Her diverse interests underscore her commitment to living a purpose-driven life.

Grounded in practical wisdom and guided by compassion, Dr. Carla McArthur remains steadfast in her mission to transform lives, serving as a reliable guide through life's challenges. For those seeking her expertise, Dr. Carla is available for motivational talks, speaking engagements, and workshops.

Contact her at (470)-207-1936 or via email at drcmcarthur@gmail.com to explore collaboration opportunities.

Don't miss out!

Visit the website below and you can sign up to receive emails whenever Dr. Carla McArthur publishes a new book. There's no charge and no obligation.

https://books2read.com/r/B-A-PGXCB-QNBUC

BOOKS 2 READ

Connecting independent readers to independent writers.

Did you love *Navigating Spiritual Suicide, A Journey to Repentance and Restoration*? Then you should read *The DREAM System, Discovering Your Life Purpose Through Faith And Action* by Carla McArthur and Dr. Carla McArthur!

Welcome to "The DREAM System: Discovering Your Life Purpose Through Faith And Action"!

In this transformative guide, the author invites you on a journey towards unlocking the life you've envisioned. A dream, like a reliable GPS, serves as a guiding force on your path to success. This book introduces the D.R.E.A.M. navigation system, a powerful tool designed to illuminate five essential keys to success.

The D.R.E.A.M System unfolds with a promise to:

Guide you towards discovering or clarifying your journey towards purpose and the life you've imagined.Motivate you to set and relentlessly pursue your goals and objectives.Navigate you through the challenges of your present circumstances.Offer you a concrete plan on how to get to where you are going.Inspire you to find and effectively manage your resources.

This isn't a quick-fix guide or an overnight life makeover. Instead, the author shares fundamental principles learned during theological studies and personal mission exploration. These principles, presented in a universally understandable way, aim to empower every reader to embark on a successful life journey.

The book acknowledges that achieving the life you imagine demands time, commitment, and inner exploration to grasp the keys to success. Each individual's choices shape their reality, and this book serves as a guide to help you make intentional choices on your journey.

Addressing the common questions of purpose and calling, the author understands the internal struggles many face. Whether you are questioning your purpose, living on purpose unintentionally, or seeking additional support, "The DREAM System" is crafted for you. It delves into battlefields and challenges conventional thinking, aiming to inspire, encourage, and empower you towards your life's destination.

Join the author on this journey of discovery and transformation, navigating through uncertainties and unveiling some of the oldest threats to success. With the goal of connecting you to your purpose, breaking away from conventional thinking, and empowering you to move forward, "The DREAM System" becomes a guide, a companion, and a source of inspiration on your path to the life you've imagined.